Teaching You How To Be Rich

Intuitive ways to become financially free and get rich

By
TIMOTHY LARSON

Table of contents

INTRODUCTION

Allow us to begin with the fundamental question of life: what does it mean to be financially free, and are there ways to attain it? Simply put, financial freedom means having all of our expenses covered without stress. But life is not that simple.

We'll try to delve a little deeper to grasp what Financial Freedom is and what the important steps are.

Having "financial freedom" implies different things to different people. However, it is commonly defined as being able to live the lifestyle of your choice while carefully managing your finances.

Financial freedom must be personal. Dream large and be specific about your objectives.

In layman's terms, financial freedom occurs when all of our costs are fulfilled, including our monthly loan payments, and we have some money left over for investing and a tiny portion saved as an emergency fund for any unexpected expenses. In a nutshell, financial freedom is having enough cash on hand to cover your living expenses. This is only possible if you are prepared. All you need is a little financial preparedness.

Most people want to be financially free. Financial freedom is often defined as having enough savings, financial assets, and cash on hand to afford the lifestyle we desire for ourselves and our families. It entails building savings that will allow us to retire or pursue the work of our choice without being constrained by a fixed annual paycheck. Financial independence is that our money works for us rather than against us.

This book will bring you to your goal of becoming financially free and stable, and various rules and ideas have been outlined in each section to help you get there!

Disclaimer ©

TIMOTHY LARSON

Chapter 1

Do You Want To Become Rich Or Sexy ??

Being sexy and being rich are two completely different things

People, including you and me, enjoy bragging about the stocks they purchased that quadrupled overnight, how much money they gained by investing in cryptocurrency, or the magical stock that will double in two months. Successful people, on the other hand, who are good and experienced with money, invest regularly in broad indices and do not touch them for years. It appears to be dull, doesn't it? You want to appear hip and seductive by discussing the next big move or forecasting the next bear market. What do you think? Being sexy and being wealthy are two wholly different things.

Three Wealth-Accumulation Laws

Being financially healthy is basic and monotonous. It is, in fact, so simple that it is difficult for others to believe it. You don't trust me. Here's the key to financial independence.

1 Set aside at least one-tenth of your earnings.

2 Invest the savings in places where your principal is safe and you may get a reasonable rent or return.

3 Do not touch it unless you have many revenue streams that fill your pockets while you sleep or travel.

Everything has a cost.

Simple, isn't it? It's not complicated. You don't have to be as informed about money as Warren Buffett to comprehend this. You don't need a finance degree to be good at it. However, relatively few people adhere to this golden rule. The reason is likewise straightforward. The principles are simple, but putting them into action is not. It takes perseverance, consistency, and guts to persevere through downturn markets while believing in oneself and the concepts. Only those who pay this price get what they paid for, which is life-changing rewards. Unfortunately, the cost of life-changing returns does not come with a price tag.

Let's speak about how to be sexy.
Enough of me telling you how boring being wealthy is. And especially since I am not a financial expert. Let's speak about the fascinating and attractive things that keep you poor that guys like me discuss the most because they generate the most views. Which stock should you invest in 2022?

Which stock can help you become a millionaire? Next month, cryptocurrency will be 10x. Have I piqued your interest? But, before I reveal any secret stocks to you, I want to make sure you understand that investing €500 or €1000 in any stock or cryptocurrency will not make you a millionaire overnight, even if it doubles in value.

Before pursuing unreasonable rewards, consider this question.

Of course, you are aware of this. What a fool I was! But, if you are aware of this, why do you pursue such unachievable goals with such a short budget? This is a question you should ask yourself every time you go out to buy a hazardous investment that someone assured you would double in a month. I mean, if you're so sure that this stock will double in value, why are you only investing $500 instead of $50,000 or even all of your money? I'll tell you why; it's because you're not confident in that investment. If you are confident, you would never invest a small sum that will make no difference in your financial situation, whether it doubles or not.

Success Guidelines

Most of you have heard of Warren Buffett, Bill Gates, and other world-famous individuals. The world's success philosophy is to discover a solid firm and then invest as much as you can in that company. As we all know, Warren Buffett is a guy of action who makes his living by taking over companies that he believes have a solid product with a rising market. Before following the enticing advice of buying a stock that will soon double in value, first, learn the concepts that have given fame and fortune to many investors. Once they are a part of your life, you will be able to make confident financial decisions. That is, the goal is not merely to accumulate riches once, but also to remain wealthy indefinitely. And if you do not modify your money habits, I can assure you that even if you suddenly accumulate a million dollars, you will lose them as quickly as you gained them.

To summarize, being attractive does not make you wealthy, and the acts that can make you wealthy are tedious. So, is wanting to look cool the cause that so many people are hurting financially? I believe it is one of the causes, as people want to be more sexy than wealthy. And I'm not just talking about folks with low incomes; I'm also talking about people with six-figure annual salaries. So they either don't invest or invest just in seductive possibilities, putting them in a position where they must labor until they die to earn a living. So, first, become wealthy by having several streams of income that fill your pockets while you sleep, and then you may choose whether or not to be sexy.

Chapter 2

Staying two steps ahead

Why do some businesses excel while others stay stagnant? The edge comes from thinking ahead. Markets are active and customers are always looking for new goods and services. With the fast growth of technology, you can achieve many things faster than you ever could. But it has also raised the desire from customers for better service. If you want to be the leader in your business, changes must be made that can keep your company relevant to the changing times.

Keeping Track with Technology

Modern gadgets can help your business run much more efficiently. The business management certification classes stress the need for businesses to adopt new technologies into their businesses, which is helping many industries collect a vast amount of data that helps them improve their goods and services. Fitness bands are helping health insurance companies to know their customers' health and lifestyle information. Keep a constant watch on future changes and how they can help move the business to the next level.

Anticipate Opportunities and Threats

Nobody can predict the future. general management school says that capable leaders will be ready for both chances and threats. A rival could go out of business and bring a sudden rise in business for your company. Are you ready to meet the higher demand? There must be plans in place for growing production ability. Certain foreign policy options could cause a slump in the market. Organizations need to have action plans to liquidate current stocks and look at different markets.

Using Business Data Effectively

A lot of data is generated by your business. Business management certification classes place a lot of importance on studying this data. It can give a lot of insight into your way of operation and offer ideas for future growth. Checking the action on the company website will show what type of users are more likely to convert quickly. That will help see you focus on those leads. Your financial info can give an idea about where money is getting lost. Controlling could improve income.

Taking Proactive Steps Against Outside Factors

Is there legislation on the table that can affect your business adversely? You can sit back and think that there is nothing that can be done about changes in the law. It is possible to believe that nothing happens quickly with the government. But that is what your peers are also doing. This is the time to think whether there is something you can do to stay out of the range of the law. There may be a chance to support your case and try to stall the passing of the law.

Summing Up!

Any online general management school can give you with the skills to think ahead like true successful do. It is imperative to spend more time analyzing future problems and possibilities instead of only managing your present business activities. All the wants of the customer cannot be met. Keep your eyes and ears open to know in advance what they might be expecting from the company in the future.

Chapter 3

Investment: Principle of building wealth

Building wealth through investment
Creating wealth is a desire that many individuals have, yet it can frequently seem like an impossible endeavor. Don't be seduced by get-rich-quick schemes and too-good-to-be-true offers that can lead you down a perilous path since achieving this objective requires patience, perseverance, and discipline.

The good news is that everyone may accumulate wealth over time by using certain guidelines and tactics. And the sooner you begin implementing these, the higher your likelihood of success.

In the paragraphs below, I've listed several important guidelines for accumulating wealth, including establishing goals and creating a strategy, investing in education and skills, managing debt, saving money, and investing it, preserving your assets, comprehending the effects of taxes, and establishing a solid credit history. We will examine each of these guidelines in more detail in this post and discuss how they can assist you in reaching your financial objectives.

1. Making a living

Starting earning money is the first thing you should do. Although it may appear simple, this step is the most important for beginners. You've probably seen graphs demonstrating how little sums of money are saved consistently and given time to grow through compound interest can eventually amount to a sizeable sum. However, those graphs never address the fundamental topic of how to start saving money.

The two main methods of earning money are earned revenue and passive income. While passive income is produced from assets, earned income is derived from the work you do for a living. It's possible that you won't start earning passive income until you've saved enough money to start investing.

These questions may help you decide what you want to accomplish and how you will get your earned income if you are either starting a career or thinking about changing careers:

- What do you like to do? Doing something you enjoy and find significant will improve your performance, help you develop a career that will last longer, and increase your chances of financial success. In fact, according to one survey, more than 90% of workers would exchange a portion of their lifetime earnings for a job that gave them more purpose.

- What are you good at? Consider your strengths and how you may make a career off of them.

What will be well paid? Consider occupations that fit what you excel at and enjoy doing and will allow you to earn the money you need. The Occupational Outlook Handbook, a yearly publication of the U.S. Bureau of Labor Statistics, is a reliable source of wage data as well as growth predictions for many industries.

- How to get there: Find out what credentials, experience, and training are necessary to pursue your desired job alternatives.

You may start on the right foot by taking these things into mind.

2. Making a plan and establishing goals

What will you do with your wealth? Do you wish to save money for your future retirement, possibly even an early one? You pay for your children's college education. Invest in a second home? Make a charitable gift from your wealth? Goal-setting is a crucial first step in accumulating wealth. You can develop a strategy to reach where you want to go when you have a clear idea of what you want to accomplish.

Establish your financial objectives first, such as paying off debt, investing for retirement, or buying a property. Be explicit on how much money you need to make each goal a reality and how long you need to do so.

Once your objectives are determined, you should create a strategy for accomplishing them. This could entail setting up a budget to encourage you to save more money, boosting your income through education or career progress, or purchasing investments that will gain value over time. Your strategy should be long-term oriented, flexible, and practical. Review your progress frequently, and adapt as necessary, to maintain moving in the right direction.

3. Budgeting

Making money on your own won't help you accumulate wealth if you wind up spending it all. Furthermore, you should put saving money above everything else if you don't have enough to cover your immediate costs (such as bills, rent, or a mortgage) or an emergency. Many experts advise having several months' worth of money saved up (for example, three to six months' worth).

Consider making these decisions to save more money for accumulating wealth:

- Keep a spending log for at least a month. Although a compact, pocket-sized notepad can work just as well, you might wish to employ financial software to assist you. Make a list of all your purchases, no matter how minor; you might be shocked to learn where your money goes.

- Trim away the excess fat. Sort the money you spend into needs and wants. The obvious needs are for clothing, food, and shelter. Health insurance payments, auto insurance if you own a car, and life insurance, if you have dependents on your income should all be added to that list. Numerous other expenses will only be wants.

- Decide how much money you want to save. As soon as you have a rough estimate of how much cash you can set aside each month, make an effort to keep to it. This does not require you to always be thrifty or live frugally.

Feel free to reward yourself and indulge (in a reasonable quantity) occasionally if you're succeeding in your savings goals. You'll feel better and have more drive to keep going.

- Set automatic saving to on. Setting up an automatic transfer of a specific amount of each paycheck into a different savings or investment account through your company or bank is a simple method to save a specific amount each month. In the same way, you can contribute to your employer's 401(k) or other retirement plan by having money deducted automatically from your paycheck. Financial advisors typically recommend making at least the minimum contribution required to receive your employer's full match.

- Search for high-yield savings. By comparing savings accounts, you may choose the ones with the best interest rates and least fees, maximizing the return on your investment. If you can afford to put away that money for several months or years, certificates of deposit (CDs) can be an excellent savings choice.

You can only reduce expenses so much, so keep that in mind as well. If your expenses are already extremely low, you should consider strategies to enhance your income.

4.Investment

Once you've managed to save some money, the following step is to invest it to increase its value. Savings are vital, but deposit accounts often offer relatively low-interest rates, and your money could eventually lose purchasing value due to inflation.

Diversification is perhaps the most crucial notion for new investors (or any investor, for that matter). To put it plainly, your aim should be to distribute your funds throughout several investment categories.

Because investments behave differently depending on the situation, this is. Bonds may be offering strong returns, for instance, if the stock market is experiencing a losing streak. Stock B might be on a tear if Stock A is experiencing a dip.

Because they invest in a variety of securities, mutual funds have some built-in diversification. Additionally, you'll benefit from better diversity if you invest in both stock and bond funds (or multiple stocks and multiple bond funds, for example), as opposed to simply one or the other.

In addition, since you'll have more time to make up for any losses if you lose money when you're younger, you can afford to take greater risks.

5. Safeguarding Your Assets
You've put a lot of effort into building your wealth and earning money. The worst-case scenario is losing everything to an

unexpected disaster. A fire could destroy your home, a car accident could result in injuries and medical costs, or a premature death could result in a loss of future income.

To protect yourself from these and other risks, insurance is a crucial component of wealth accumulation. In the event of a fire, your home and possessions will be replaced by your home insurance; in the event of an automobile accident, your vehicle insurance will make you whole; and in the event of an early death, your life insurance will give your beneficiaries a death benefit. Another sort of policy that will replace your income if you are hurt, ill, or otherwise rendered unable of working is long-term disability insurance. Since insurance policies tend to get more expensive as you get older, even young, healthy people should think about them. Because of this, purchasing life insurance when you are 25 years old and unmarried may be far more cost-effective than when you are 10 years older and have a partner, kids, and a mortgage. Deed

Chapter 4

Becoming Financially free

Everyone has experienced the panic that descends over them upon seeing the cost of an unforeseen auto repair. How are we going to cover that expense? What if, though, a car repair was only a little inconvenience? You pay the bill without second-guessing without fear. You no longer remember it a week later! It has a negligible impact on your financial status. No emergency exists. Not even a hiccup!

Do you experience any relief? Financial freedom feels like that.

Financial Freedom: What Is It?

Financial independence allows you to make decisions without being unduly concerned about how those choices may affect your finances. This is because you are financially ready for everything life throws at you—you have no debt, cash in the bank, and you're making investments for the future.

In other words, you are in charge of your finances rather than having them in charge of you. You have choices when you have financial freedom, or as we like to call it, financial serenity. You don't need to worry about whether your finances will allow you to replace your water heater or purchase groceries for a single mother who has lost her job.

How to Obtain Financial Independence

The road to financial independence is not a quick-rich scheme. Furthermore, being financially independent does not absolve you of the obligation to manage your money wisely. The exact opposite. Complete financial management is the consequence of effort, sacrifice, and patience. And the effort was worthwhile.

Here are some ways you can start moving toward financial independence right away:

1.Learn How to Budget

You won't go ahead if you don't have a financial strategy. Instead, you'll be left wondering where your money went at the end of each month! That is not financial freedom; rather, it is a recipe for financial ruin.

Financial freedom is unattainable if you do not live on a budget. You must direct your money's movement or you will be left wondering where it went. Before the month begins, assign each dollar a purpose and keep track of your spending. If you routinely overspend or underspend in some areas, you may easily modify the amount in those categories.

Budgeting is essential for getting your money in order, but it doesn't stop there. Even if you reach financial independence, you will still create a new budget each month. You need a plan regardless of your financial situation.

Nobody wins the major championship game by accident, and you won't get to financial freedom by chance either. Budgeting is the first step toward intentionally accumulating wealth. Begin budgeting with confidence and take control of your money today.

2. Eliminate Debt from Your Life— Forever

If you have debt, such as credit cards, student loans, or vehicle loans, it's time to get rid of it. Why? Because as long as you're transferring hundreds of dollars in debt payments to banks and lenders every month, you'll never truly feel financial freedom.

Your income is your most potent wealth-building weapon. And you won't be able to meet your financial objectives if all you have to work with are scraps left over after paying credit card bills and student loan installments.

Paying off your debts allows you to create the groundwork for long-term wealth accumulation. Before you begin fighting your debt, make sure you have $1,000 set up for emergencies. You don't want an unexpected expense to interrupt your progress.

When they start budgeting, most people feel like they got a pay boost, which is great news for you. Spend all of your spare money on your smallest debt until it is gone. Then keep the snowball moving. Paying off debt is difficult, but nothing beats the satisfaction of really keeping the money you earn each month.

Are you ready to embark on your debt-free journey? Then sign up for Financial Peace University, the education that has helped millions of individuals just like you get out (and stay out) of debt!

3. Establish financial objectives

Everyone desires financial independence. It's a wonderful dream! But a dream without a goal is just a desire. That is why defining financial objectives, such as getting out of debt or preparing for retirement, is critical on your path to financial freedom. They provide you with something to aim for!

How do you know if you have a decent objective to pursue? Here's how to set goals that truly work:

Be specific.
Make your goals measurable.
Set a time limit for yourself.
Make sure they are your own.
Make a list of your objectives.
Let's say you genuinely want to get out of debt. That's a good goal to have, but it's not enough. How much debt do you want to pay off? Is it $20,000? Now we're getting somewhere! When do you want to be debt-free? How to do 12 months sound? Done!

And just like that, you have a personal, measurable goal with a fixed deadline: I want to pay off $20,000 in debt in 12 months. All you have to do now is write it down and keep it in front of you as you pursue it.

4. Make a wise career choice.

Your income, as previously said, is your most powerful wealth-building weapon. So there's a lot at stake when it comes to choosing a career. Don't stay at a dead-end job, especially if it's making you unhappy. Find a profession you enjoy that also supports your financial goals so you may enjoy the ride.

So, what should you look for? Here are a few things to bear in mind:

Where do you want to be in ten years? Begin with the end in mind. Is this employment in line with your long-term goals?
Is there earning potential? Even if you're not earning your ideal wage right away, make

sure there's room for growth as your worth grows.

Can you grow? Are there opportunities for you to advance and grow personally and professionally?

Do you like your job? Don't waste your career doing something you despise. Find something you're enthusiastic about that allows you to put your talents and skills to use.

Do the perks support your financial independence goals? Your alternatives for retirement savings and health insurance can have a significant impact on your ability to generate wealth.

Take your work choices seriously because they can have a significant impact on your long-term financial plan. Want to know more about finding and doing work that pays well and has a huge impact? Check out Ken Coleman's latest book, From Paycheck to Purpose: The Clear Path to Doing Work You Love!

5. Put money aside for emergencies

If financial freedom is your objective, you must have a fully loaded emergency fund. It functions as a buffer between you and the unforeseen life events that we all face, such as auto repairs, broken appliances, and medical expenses. That's why, once you're out of debt, you should raise your emergency fund to cover 3-6 months of costs.

Having funds on hand to handle an unexpected life event gives you peace of mind and is an important aspect of your overall financial plan. When you have a completely funded savings account, you will notice a difference in your budget. You'll be free to say yes to shopping sprees and specialty lattes with no guilt!

6. Plan for Large Purchases

Because you're not taking on debt, you'll also need a savings plan for large purchases that aren't emergencies.

Consider summer vacation. It's that easy! Create a line item in your monthly budget and divide the entire cost of your vacation by the number of months you have to save. You're no longer in debt, so you can enjoy your vacation without worrying about a credit card bill following you home.

You'll have the financial basis to begin investing after you have a fully funded emergency fund and a plan in place to cover large purchases.

7. Plan for Your Retirement Now

Now that you've established a strategy for short-term savings, you're ready to work with a financial advisor to maximize your long-term investment alternatives. The good news is that the sooner you begin investing, the longer your money has to grow. That is the power of compound growth in action. Here's where to begin:

Begin by taking advantage of any tax-favored retirement funds offered by your employer, such as your 401(k) or 403(b). According to The National Study of Millionaires, eight out of ten millionaires invested in their company's 401(k) plan, which aided their financial success.

How much money should you put aside? Invest 15% of your earnings in retirement. And, if your employer matches your 401(k) contributions, take advantage of it! Don't turn down free money.

If your company offers a Roth 401(k) with solid mutual fund alternatives, that's fantastic! You can put your entire 15% there. However, if you have a standard 401(k), invest up to the match, then invest the remaining 15% in a Roth IRA. Return to your 401(k) if you still have some of your 15% remaining after maxing out your Roth IRA.

Why is a Roth a good investment? When you invest in a Roth 401(k) or a Roth IRA, your money grows tax-free. That is, when you withdraw money in retirement, you do not have to pay taxes on it. That is a significant benefit you should not overlook.

8. Look for Money-Saving Opportunities

If you haven't taken a close look at what you're spending your money on each month, now is the time to do so!

It's easy to get caught up in life's hustle and bustle and forget about that gym ticket you signed up for at the start of the year but haven't used it in months. Or all those streaming services you signed up for even though you only watch a few hours of television every week.

Here are a few quick methods to save money right now:

Buy generic instead of name brand.

Plan your meals and bring leftovers to work.

You may make your coffee at home.

Subscriptions and memberships can be paused or canceled.

Reduce your energy use.

Make use of cashback apps and coupons.

What's more, guess what? Even after achieving financial freedom, more than 93% of millionaires still utilize coupons to save money on their purchases. It turns out that saving money is a tough habit to break!

9. Live Inside Your Means

To put it another way, you must live on less than you make. This is linked to having a budget. To achieve financial freedom, you must be self-disciplined and ready to say no to some things you can't afford to buy right now to save more in the long run.

We're not suggesting it's terrible to have things or seek pleasant things. We just don't want you to have your stuff. When you spend money you don't have on a car or a house to impress people you don't even like, you'll find yourself trapped in a vicious circle of debt and overspending. That is hardly a prescription for financial freedom. The opposite is true.

10. Assist Your Children in Saving for College

If you already give 15% of your salary to retirement and wish to start saving for your children's college, you can do so by investing in an Education Savings Account ESA.

The money you donate to an ESA, like a Roth IRA, grows tax-free, which means you won't have to pay taxes on it when it's used to pay for college costs. You can currently pay up to $2,000 per year for each child in an ESA. Income limits do exist, and your financial advisor may help you determine if they apply to you.2

If you wish to save more than an ESA allows (or if you don't qualify for one), talk to your financial expert about a 529 plan. These services are also tax-free! Just be aware that there are some 529 plans to avoid. Prepaid tuition plans and fixed investment choices should be avoided.3

The beautiful thing about saving for your children's education is that by assisting them in avoiding student debt, you are also preparing them for financial freedom!

11. Pay Off Your Mortgage Early

There's a reason the average billionaire pays off their house in roughly 10 years.4 Think about it: What would your life look like without a mortgage payment? When you own your house (not the bank or your debt lender), the grass under your feet just feels different. That is freedom. financial freedom.

Making an extra house payment every quarter might help you pay off your property years ahead of schedule and save you tens of thousands of dollars in interest costs. You can use a mortgage payoff tool to figure out how to shorten your mortgage term.

12. Make Your Health a Priority

We all know a healthy diet and routine exercise are important for your health. But what if we told you a healthy lifestyle is great for your bank account too?

There's little question that we have a health problem in America today. And ill health could cost you your financial independence if you don't do anything to handle it. That's because greater health problems mean more doctor appointments and more bills, and that leads to higher insurance premiums.

The annual expense of treating different diseases caused by poor diet is around $300 per person or $50 billion nationally.5 And roughly 1 in 10 people in the U.S. today owe some type of medical debt—that's 23 million Americans with medical debt totaling close to $200 billion.6

When you take care of your physical, mental, and spiritual health, you're also taking care of your financial health as well. Another study showed that if U.S. adults followed a healthy diet, decreases in heart disease, cancer, Type 2 diabetes, and Alzheimer's disease could amount to $88.2 billion in cost savings

13. Obtain the Appropriate Insurance

You may be wondering, "What does insurance have to do with financial freedom? A lot! When you look at championship-winning sports teams, you'll notice that they don't just focus on offense— they also have a strong defense. That is what insurance is: a defensive strategy that saves you money.

Without the proper insurance, a horrible accident or a lawsuit might jeopardize all you've fought so hard for. While planning, saving, and investing will get you there, insurance will keep you there.

Here are eight types of insurance that you must have:

Life insurance for the short term

Automobile insurance

Insurance for homeowners and renters

Health coverage

Assurance for long-term disability

Insurance for long-term care

Identity theft defense

Umbrella Insurance

14. Consult a Financial Advisor

The idea of actively making financial and financial choices might be scary. You are not alone if you feel this way.

Take note that you've worked hard to establish the proper foundation, so don't gamble with your financial future! You require the expertise of a financial advisor to help you manage your investment options and weather the ups and downs of your money.

A financial advisor can assist you in the following ways:

Make decisions about your investment plan.

Rebalance your money regularly to reduce risk.

Create a realistic plan for financial freedom for yourself.

Understand your financial options outside of retirement funds.

Create a withdrawal strategy for your situation.

15.Be Generous to Others.

Financial freedom entails more than simply being able to handle unforeseen expenses, such as automobile repairs, without breaking a sweat. The pleasure begins when you realize you can meet the needs of others. Consider assisting a needy family by paying for their automobile repair! It's no longer just about you—it's about leaving a legacy!

The best aspect is that you don't have to wait till you have the financial independence to be generous. Even if you're focused on paying off debt or building an emergency fund, we recommend starting your budget with a line item for giving. At that point, your contribution may appear to be tithing to a local church or charity. But after you've achieved financial independence, you may go wild with giving!

If you live like no one else, you will be able to live and give like no one else. It's well worth the work it takes to get there. You can do it.

Chapter 5

Improving your financial health

5 Rules to Improve Your Financial Health

These general ideas can assist you in achieving specific objectives.

Your financial health is affected by all of your financial decisions and behaviors. It's always a good idea to think about what we should be doing in general to enhance our financial health and habits. Here, we'll go over five general personal finance rules that will help you start on track to reach any financial goals you have.

1. Calculate Your Net Worth and Personal Budget

Money comes in and money leaves. For many people, this is as far as their awareness of personal finances goes. Rather than neglecting your finances and leaving them to chance, a little number crunching can assist you in evaluating your present financial health and determining how to achieve your short- and long-term financial goals.

● Determine Your Net Worth

As a starting point, determine your net worth—the difference between what you own and what you owe. To begin calculating your net worth, make a list of your assets (what you possess) and liabilities (what you owe). Then, remove the liabilities from the assets to determine your net worth.

Your net worth reflects your current financial situation, and it is common for the value to fluctuate over time. Calculating your net worth once can be useful, but the true benefit comes from doing so on a regular (at least yearly) basis. Tracking your net worth over time helps you to assess your development, highlight your achievements, and discover areas for growth.

- **Age-Related Net Worth**

Age has a significant impact on net worth. Younger investors are more likely to have a low or negative net worth when they begin their careers, but older investors have a significantly higher net worth later in their careers.

- **Making a Personal Budget**

Creating a personal budget or spending plan is also essential. A personal budget, whether created monthly or annually, is an important financial tool because it can help you plan for future costs, limit excessive spending, save for future goals, and prioritize where you put your money.

There are several techniques to building a personal budget, but all include calculating income and cost predictions. Your budget's revenue and expense categories will be determined by your situation and may change over time. The following are examples of common income levels:

Alimony Bonuses
Child maintenance
Disability compensation
Dividends and interest
Royalties and rents
Pension income
Salaries/wages
Social Security Suggestions
Among the general expense categories are:

Childcare/eldercare

Payments on debt (auto loan, school loan, credit card)

Tuition, daycare, books, and materials

Sports, hobbies, literature, movies, DVDs, concerts, and streaming services are all sources of entertainment and pleasure.

Food (groceries and eating out)

Birthdays, holidays, and charitable contributions

Housing (mortgage or rent, upkeep)

Health, home/renters, auto, and life insurance

Medical/Health Care (doctor visits, dentist visits, prescription drugs, and other known costs)

Personal expenses (clothing, hair care, gym membership, professional dues)

Savings (for retirement, schooling, an emergency fund, or specific goals like a vacation)

Weddings, anniversaries, graduations, and bar/bat mitzvahs are examples of special occasions.

Transport (gasoline, taxis, metro, tolls, and parking)
Utilities (phone, electric, water, gas, cell phone, cable television, internet)

 A budget is only useful if it is adhered to. Track your income and expenditure across categories after you've created a personal budget. Then, based on what transpired, fine-tune your budget.
Subtract your expenses from your income after you've completed the necessary predictions. If you have any extra cash, you can have a surplus, and you can choose how to spend, save, or invest it. If your spending surpasses your income, you must change your budget by either raising your income (working more hours or taking on a second job) or decreasing your expenses.

2. Identify and Control Lifestyle Inflation
Most people will spend more money if they had more money. As people advance in their jobs and earn better salaries, they tend

to spend more, a phenomenon known as "lifestyle inflation."

Even if you can pay your payments, lifestyle inflation can be detrimental in the long run since it inhibits your potential to accumulate wealth. Every dollar you spend now equals less money later and during retirement, and having more disposable income today does not ensure having more money afterward.

Some rise in spending is natural as your career and personal circumstances evolve. You could need to improve your wardrobe to dress suitably for a new job, or you might require a larger house as your family expands. With more obligations at work, you may decide that hiring someone to mow the grass or clean the house makes sense, freeing up time to spend with family and friends and increasing your quality of life.

Re-evaluate your budget as you progress through life stages to ensure that it reflects the proper conditions in your life. When making a list of your expenses, consider which costs are genuinely necessary and which might be eliminated.

Consider what changes you would make if you received a pay decrease at work. How would a 20% reduction in your income affect your spending or saving?

3. Recognize Needs vs. Wants—and Spend With Intention

It's in your best interest to understand the distinction between "needs" and "wants." Food, shelter, healthcare, transportation, and a reasonable amount of clothing are examples of necessities. It's also crucial to set aside money for savings each month, albeit this is far more dependent on your other demands being addressed first.

Wants, on the other hand, are items you'd want to have but don't need for survival. These expenditures may be so ingrained in our daily lives that they appear to be necessities. Wants are non-essential products, such as a streaming subscription that isn't vital for survival or foregoing a morning treat that has become part of your daily routine.

When there is no specified degree of either, the border between "wants" and "needs" becomes blurred. An automobile is an excellent example. You might be able to argue that a car is a "want" depending on your city's public transit. However, what style of car is acceptable for the many of us who consider it a "need"? What is a reasonable trade-off between a larger car payment and a fancier vehicle?

Your budget should prioritize your necessities. You should only spend your discretionary income on wants when your needs have been addressed. Again, if you have money left over after paying for the things you need each week or month, you don't have to spend it all.

Saving money for the future is necessary as long as your immediate bodily necessities are covered (food, shelter, transportation). Furthermore, some may claim that receiving a 401(k) match from your work is a top priority.

4. Begin saving early.

It is sometimes stated that it is never too late to begin saving for retirement. That is technically correct, but the sooner you begin, the better off you will be in your retirement years. This is due to the ability of compounding.

Compounding is the reinvestment of money, and it works best over time. The longer earnings are reinvested, the bigger the value of the investment and the larger (hypothetical) earnings will be.

The Compounding Effect
Compounding was dubbed "the eighth wonder of the world" by Einstein once he realized its ability to generate wealth.

To demonstrate the necessity of starting early, suppose you wish to save $1,000,000 by the age of 60 and expect to earn 5% interest every year.

If you begin saving at the age of 20, you would need to contribute $655 per month for 40 years—a total of $314,544—to become a millionaire by the age of 60.
If you begin saving at the age of 40, you must contribute $2,433 every month for a total of $583,894 over 20 years.
If you begin saving at the age of 50, you must contribute $6,440 a month for a total of $772,786 over ten years.
The sooner you begin, the easier it will be to achieve your long-term financial objectives. To achieve the same goal in the future, you

will need to save less each month and contribute less total.

5. Create and Keep an Emergency Fund

An emergency fund is exactly what the name implies: money set aside for emergencies. The fund is designed to assist you in paying for items that would not ordinarily be included in your budget. This covers unforeseen costs like auto repairs or a trip to the dentist. It may also assist you in meeting your usual expenses if your income is stopped.

Although the typical recommendation is to save three to six months' worth of living expenses in an emergency fund, the unpleasant reality is that this amount is sometimes insufficient for many people to meet a large expense or withstand a loss of income. Most people should attempt to save at least six months' worth of living expenses—more if possible—in today's unpredictable economic situation.

Remember that developing an emergency backup is a continuous mission. You will very certainly require it as soon as it is funded. Instead of getting disheartened, be grateful that you were financially prepared and restart the fund-building process

.

Chapter 6

Living the living the life

**Amazing things you can do if
you're Financially Free**

Financial success is a significant
aim for many people. Being
financially independent is one
method to accomplish this. Financial
independence needs a high level of
focus and determination over a long

period. It could imply that you are not spending as much money as you would otherwise. You could start to wonder if it's worth the effort, or if you should just live in the moment.

Whether this is already a goal of yours and you need a motivational boost, or you're considering embarking on this journey, we thought we'd help inspire you by sharing some of the fantastic things you can do if you're financially free.

1.Stop working or reduce your workload

The most significant advantage of achieving financial independence is not being bound to a 9 to 5 work and being a part of the rat race. You now have the freedom to choose how you spend your time once you have achieved financial independence. Previously, you may have worked because you needed the money, but today you may work on your own terms. This could mean working part-time, not working at all, or perhaps changing occupations to something you would love a lot more.

2. Plan your adventure / travel the world

The world has so much to offer, whether it's experiencing stunning scenery, learning about new cultures embarking on unforgettable adventures. We asked our Sprive team what their ideal adventure would be, and here are some of their top suggestions.

Go to Antarctica.
Visit 5 different volcanoes throughout the world.
Climb Everest and bungee jump on every continent
Trek through Japan's Sagano Bamboo Forest.
Take a three-month safari adventure.
Spend a year in a distant nation.
Dolphin swimming
Scuba diving
Take care of your health.
You've worked hard to get to this financial position, whether it's through long hours at work or days

spent researching which investments to make. Now is the moment to prioritize your mental and physical health.

The immediate benefit is not having to worry about money and the associated stress relief. You may spend more time relaxing while also keeping your body active by engaging in activities that you enjoy.

3. Volunteering
Many people often reflect on their lives and wonder if they have made a difference in the world. Have you done anything to improve someone's life materially? Being in a financially secure situation allows you to make charitable

contributions. You can even volunteer your time and skills to support a charity and make a meaningful difference for a cause you care about.

4. Devote time to your passions.

Do you have any hobbies that you would like to pursue but have never had the time? Whether it's golf or squash, music, wine tasting, or cooking, the objective is to do something you love as much as you can. Who wouldn't want to spend their time doing what they enjoy?

You can also attempt new interests that you might not have tried otherwise. Again, we asked the Sprive crew what new activities they would explore, and here are some of their suggestions.

Martial arts - strive for a black belt
Photography entails being able to take stunning photographs.
Brew beer - I enjoy making tasty beer.
Play golf and be good at it for a change.
Maybe I'll go antique shopping and find that one-of-a-kind item.
Create my artwork by painting
Learn to dance, perhaps a little Salsa or Tango.
Relationships
Spending more time with the people that matter the most to you in the world. This might be family members or friends with whom you

have not spent as much time as you would like. With more control over your time, you can spend it meeting new friends or reconnecting with existing ones with whom you have lost touch.

5.Train others

One way you might give back is to teach others how you achieved financial independence. It can be tremendously fulfilling to use your experience to help others succeed.

Make your money grow
You've achieved financial independence, but why stop there? You can continue to invest your time in increasing your wealth, enhancing your lifestyle, and increasing your

financial buffer. This can be accomplished by diversifying your investment portfolio, investing in real estate, and exploring other side hustles that you did not have the opportunity to pursue earlier in your work by taking use of the time you have.

Remember that obtaining financial freedom does not necessitate spending a lot of money. Simply said, it means having the resources and flexibility to live the life you desire on your terms.

6. Pay off your debt

Becoming financially independent makes a key step towards paying off debt and improving your overall financial health. It can provide you with more income and the discipline necessary to create and stick to a budget, allowing you to allocate more money towards paying off debts - be it your student loan debt or your car loan.

You can also prioritize debt repayment as a top financial goal and avoid new debts by living within your means and making wise financial decisions. Additionally, building a good credit score by making timely payments on your debts can help you negotiate better payment terms and lower interest rates with your lenders. By committing to paying off your debts, you can regain control over your finances and start saving money for your long-term goals, such as retirement or buying a home.

6. Go back to school or pursue further education

You may find that pursuing further education is a fulfilling way to use your newfound freedom. The decision to return to school can be motivated by several factors, including a desire to learn a new skill or trade, a passion for a particular subject or career, or the potential for increased earning power.

For some, going back to school may represent an opportunity for personal growth and development, while for others, it may be a strategic investment in their future. Additionally, pursuing education may also provide networking opportunities and connect with like-minded individuals, opening up new avenues for personal and professional growth. Ultimately, the decision to go back to school or pursue further education will depend on individual goals and motivations, and the potential benefits of doing so.

7. Give back to your community

You might have a strong motivation to give back to your community by supporting local businesses or initiatives. Financial freedom provides the opportunity to pursue more fulfilling goals, and supporting local businesses and initiatives is one way to do that.

Not only does supporting local businesses contribute to the growth and well-being of the community, but it can also create a sense of social responsibility and personal satisfaction. Additionally, it can help promote a sense of community and can have positive economic impacts by creating jobs and encouraging more spending within the local economy. Financial freedom can provide you with the means to make a real difference in your community, and supporting local businesses and initiatives can be a meaningful way to do so.

8.Write a book

If you were financially free, one motivation for writing a book could be to share your knowledge, experiences, or stories with others. You may have a unique perspective or valuable insights that you want to share with the world, and writing a book can be a great way to do so.

Additionally, writing a book can be a creative outlet that allows you to explore your interests and passions, and it can be a fulfilling accomplishment in itself. Depending on the topic and genre of your book, you may also have the potential to impact and inspire others, further contributing to your sense of purpose and fulfillment. Writing a book can be a challenging and time-consuming process, but if you are financially free, you may have the freedom and resources to pursue this endeavor without the financial constraints that often limit writers.

9. Spend more time outdoors

Perhaps you like to spend more time enjoying the outdoors. Many people are drawn to outdoor activities like hiking, camping, and fishing as a way to relax, unwind, and connect with nature. Being financially free could give you the freedom to explore new outdoor hobbies or to travel to beautiful natural areas around the world.

Additionally, spending more time outdoors has been shown to have a range of health benefits, from reducing stress and anxiety to improving cardiovascular health. By pursuing outdoor activities, you may be able to improve your physical and mental well-being, while also developing a deeper appreciation for the natural world.

10. Buy your dream house

Owning a dream house can offer a sense of pride, accomplishment, and stability. It can also provide you with the space and amenities that you need to enjoy your hobbies, interests, and relationships.

For example, you might choose a dream house with a large backyard to host barbecues with friends and family, or a property with an amazing view to indulge your passion for surfing. A dream house can also be an excellent investment opportunity that can potentially appreciate over time.

If you have financial freedom, you can choose a dream house that truly represents your aspirations and creates a comfortable and enjoyable home environment.

11. Establish a trust to aid future generations.

For those who have attained financial freedom, building trust to assist future generations can be a strong motivator. Trusts can be used to preserve and distribute wealth across several generations, guaranteeing that upcoming generations of family members will have the means to prosper.

Using trusts, people can leave a lasting legacy that transcends material wealth by communicating their beliefs and charitable aspirations to future generations.

By creating trust, people can ensure that their fortune is used to benefit the causes and people they care about while also trusting the long-term financial security of their loved ones. For individuals who are able to do so, setting up a trust to support future generations can be a way to leave a constructive legacy for future generations and to have a lasting impact on the world.

12. A reserve fund

Gaining financial freedom requires you to save money for unforeseen expenses that contour financial plans. This money is collected in an emergency fund. The recommended amount for an emergency fund is three to six months' worth of costs, and it should be stored in a separate account that is accessible but unconnected to regular spending. Having this safety net allows you to avoid incurring debt to pay for unforeseen costs like auto repairs or medical expenses. This also gives you a feeling of financial security, which can aid in focusing on reaching your long-term financial objectives, like paying off your student loan debt.

13. Establish your own company.

You might have an entrepreneurial spirit and desire to make your passion your full-time job. Alternatively, perhaps you want to start a company that shares your beliefs and has a positive influence on your neighborhood or the entire world.

Financial independence can give one the time and resources required to invest in starting a business from scratch without having to worry about urgent financial responsibilities. The ability to take chances and explore opportunities that might not have been possible otherwise can be provided by being financially free.

A sense of independence, creativity, and fulfillment that may be challenging to find in regular work can also be provided by owning a business.

14. Invest in a sports automobile

Purchasing a sports car can be something you think about doing if you enjoy driving. Owning a sports car may be a source of tremendous satisfaction for some people since it represents success and accomplishment.

In addition, driving a sports automobile can be an exciting and entertaining experience.

Owning a high-performance car can be a dream come true for automotive aficionados, and having financial independence may make that goal a reality. It's crucial to keep in mind, too, that owning a sports car has obligations and expenses in addition to the one-time investment, such as upkeep, insurance, and fuel bills.

Therefore, before making the decision to purchase a sports automobile, it is crucial to thoroughly weigh the actual expenses and prospective advantages of doing so.

15. Sample different cuisines

Are you a foodie? You might feel inspired to experiment with different foods and enjoy good dining. Financial independence would allow you to travel to different countries to experience local cuisine or dine at upscale establishments that you might have previously thought were beyond of your price range.

Foodies may also use their financial independence to experiment in their kitchens with various products and preparation methods.

Financial independence can enable you to pursue your passion for food and discover the culinary world in fascinating new ways, whether you choose to make a reservation at a Michelin-starred restaurant or try a new street food seller.

16. Go to festivals and concerts

A significant motivator can be the opportunity to take in the ambiance, enjoy live music, and make lifelong memories.

Financial independence enables you to attend the concerts and festivals of your choice by traveling to other cities or nations and purchasing expensive tickets. Whether you enjoy jazz, classical, rock, or pop music, there is something for everyone.

Events and festivals centered around music can be a great way to meet new people, celebrate diversity, and take in the best performances by well-known performers. You can also sample the local food, delve into the area's cultural attractions, and go on new adventures.

Purchase cosmetic procedures or other beauty services.

Everyone has various motives and objectives, and for some people, getting cosmetic surgery or other forms of aesthetic care may be a top priority if they had unlimited funds. Cosmetic surgery may be chosen by some people to increase their self-esteem, improve some undesirable physical traits, or just to improve their appearance.

Others may choose non-invasive procedures to take care of their skin, unwind, and relax, such as facials, massages, and other aesthetic procedures.

It is ultimately up to the person to choose what makes them happy and confident in their skin, even though there are undoubtedly good arguments for and against pursuing these treatments.

17. Host gatherings and parties

There are several reasons why you might desire to host gatherings and events. Some people may see it as an opportunity to mingle and spend time with friends and family. You can cultivate connections and establish relationships by bringing individuals from many walks of life together through the hosting of events and gatherings.

Additionally, hosting parties and events can be a way to give back to your community by providing a place for people to gather and enjoy themselves. Whatever your motivations, being financially free can provide the means and flexibility to make your party and event dreams a reality